I0820951

GRACIOUS HOME

Cultivating a Spirit of Welcome

GRACIOUS HOME

Cultivating a Spirit of Welcome

MELISSA LESTER

Hoffman Media
2323 2nd Avenue North
Birmingham, AL 35203
hoffmanmedia.com

ISBN #979-8-9913469-0-0
Printed in China

FLOWERS

CONTENTS

FOREWORD

When I met Melissa Lester during my tenure as Artist-in-Residence for *Victoria* magazine, I was almost immediately struck by the authentic way in which she lives out the ideals of gracious living. So many of us aspire to these ideals, but here was a woman who embodies them. I would, thus, be hard-pressed to think of anyone more well-suited to write a book intended to capture the very essence of a word too easily taken for granted: *home*.

You will find in these pages that it is a thoughtful heart that makes for the gracious home and that one can cultivate a place of belonging for family and a spirit of welcome for guests long before the wallpaper is up, antiques are collected, and decorating is finished.

Jacqueline Kennedy Onassis loved to send beautiful books to her friends and once wrote on a card enclosed, "This is an 'escape' book." Such is this lovely new volume by my dear friend Melissa—an escape book that will pair most beautifully with a warm cup of tea as we dream of cultivating a sense of place for those we love and a spirit of welcome for all who cross our thresholds.

Jenny Bohannon

COVE COTTAGE

"There's never a pleasant, sunlit road
In all the ways we roam
Like the little, narrow, familiar street
That runs by the door of home."

—Esther M. Clark Hill

A Place of Belonging

There is perhaps no word in the English language more full of longing and tenderness than *home*. Opportunity may find us visiting the most beautiful destinations in the world—seeking repose amid the pampering environs of luxury hotels, surveying breathtaking landscapes of misty moors and rolling fields of heather, and even exploring the castles of kings and queens—but nothing surpasses the incomparable comfort of stepping into one's own cottage. Weary travelers feel drawn to it as to a cherished quilt. Wherever the path leads and however far we wander, the warming glow of a waiting porch light on the other side of the journey serves as a beacon that guides us to return.

No matter how humble the dwelling or how snug its proportions, the spaces that shelter our most cherished dreams also hold our hearts. Thinking back to the earliest memories of my childhood bedrooms, I remember walls the color of sunshine, windows framed by billowing curtains in a pastel gingham print, and a "magical" naptime blanket that seemed to know instinctively whether I needed a cooling touch or a warm embrace. My cache of treasures included porcelain dolls, ceramic angels, and a delicate tea set, all hand-painted by my paternal grandmother. The bedside table brimmed with classics such as *A Little Princess* and *The Secret Garden*, while its single drawer held the scribblings of my very first handwritten stories.

My younger sister and I shared this haven, but we often took turns in serving as hostess. Jennifer and I whiled away many an afternoon planning parties for one another, baking tiny cakes in our toy oven and serving the sprinkle-topped confections at the Apple Table, a pint-sized piece named for its colorful fruit motifs. During those playful teatimes, we sipped hot water from paper cups but tasted the pure refreshment of hospitality. Even as little girls, we experienced the joy of filling a space with love and sharing it with someone special.

As decades pass, I grow more nostalgic for the houses where I grew up, as well as the memories made there with my parents and siblings. "One's home is like a delicious piece of pie you order in a restaurant on a country road one cozy evening—the best piece of pie you have ever eaten in your life—and can never find again," writes Lemony Snicket. "After you leave home, you may find yourself feeling homesick, even if you have a new home that has nicer wallpaper and a more efficient dishwasher than the one you grew up in." Although we moved several times during my youth, with my mother's knack for decorating, each new location very quickly felt like home.

Akin to details captured in the snapshots that line our old photo albums, I see in flashes of memory items that bring to mind each member of the family: my mother's china cabinet arranged with blue-and-white wares; the polished wooden desk where my father, a minister, worked on his sermons amid stacks of books; and a shifting kaleidoscope of playthings once held dear by my younger sister and brother. Many of these objects, now bestowed from one generation to the next, continue to whisper the tales of long ago—stories that seem to grow sweeter in the retelling.

As I matured, other dwellings took up residence in my heart. My first dorm room, confirmed by my roommate to be the smallest one on campus, still occupies a place larger than its measurements, thanks to a creative arrangement of furniture, the petal-strewn Laura Ashley ensemble that graced my bed, and many hours of late-night conversation with girls on our hall. When I married after college, my husband and I discovered new delights in each place we lived. Joe carried me across the threshold of a duplex. Its spacious kitchen bore witness to my first forays into cooking. (How I wish those ample cabinets could have counseled me that the "sweet milk" called for in the classic chicken pot pie recipe I attempted was actually milk and not the sweetened condensed milk that I used in preparing the crust!)

After a few more years of renting, along with several hard-earned lessons in the culinary arts, housekeeping, and the like, we purchased our first property. This was a step we took prayerfully, approaching the milestone with great intention. Joe and I asked for God's blessing over our home and for Him to give us a heart for welcoming others to it.

I still remember the joy of turning the key to that Cape Cod charmer. Running my hands over the walls, I marveled at the possibilities for making them our own with paint and wallpaper—a new freedom we fully embraced. We worked tirelessly over the next few months to make each space and surface our own.

In fulfillment of our hopes, we found many opportunities to practice hospitality. By this time, I had mastered a few simple meals and enjoyed inviting guests to our table for Sunday lunch, a dinner party, or afternoon tea. We hosted Thanksgiving for our extended families—given my previous blunder with chicken pot pie, I literally made the entire menu in a trial run—and we discovered time and again the joy of connecting with loved ones during holidays, special occasions, and casual gatherings. The most exciting welcome, by far, came in bringing our newborn baby boy home to that sweet cottage.

As our family expanded to include four children, our housing needs grew as well. Through the years, we have moved several times, drawing close in the cozy quarters of an urban apartment and spreading out in the airy environs of a sprawling woodland oasis. Our abodes have comprised a mix of large and small spaces, prized heirlooms and timeworn pieces, well-kept areas and neglected corners. The sizes of our homes have gone up and down, and so have resources such as time, income, and physical abilities.

My purpose in sharing these reflections, besides revealing a bit of my personal story, is to underscore my belief that the place where you abide is home. Whether your world exists fully within four walls or extends to vast real estate holdings, cultivating an atmosphere of welcome is a worthy aim. Within these pages, I hope you will find encouragement for creating a place of belonging—one that nurtures the spirits of all who enter. As poet Oliver Wendell Holmes Sr. extolled, "Where we love is home, home that our feet may leave, but not our hearts."

BALANCING ASPIRATIONS AND INSPIRATION

One of the great privileges of my life is serving as the editor of *Victoria*. The publication proposes a return to loveliness and delivers on that promise with well-appointed interiors, charming travel destinations, artful entertaining, and thoughtful text. I discovered the magazine as a newlywed, and its sense of romance spoke directly to my heart. In those days, we were scraping by on my entry-level publishing salary while my husband finished school. Each issue transported me from our tiny, one-bedroom duplex to the streets of Paris or villages in the English countryside.

Poring over the pages, I dreamed of the distant someday when Joe and I would be able to fill our home with beautiful antiques like the ones I so admired. Imagine my surprise to spy an elegantly dressed bed strewn with a rosy comforter—the very one that I had saved my pennies to purchase before our wedding. This serendipitous connection showed me that even as a young woman of modest means, I could embody the essence of *Victoria*.

29

I cherished that issue for many years because it reminded me that gracious living, in many ways, is a state of the heart.

This volume brims with the gorgeous photos that subscribers have come to expect from the magazine. Many of these images take shape through the contributions of a variety of staff members, from test-kitchen chefs developing recipes to prop stylists arranging vignettes and photographers capturing perfect shots. Other professionals, such as interior designers and artists, lend their talents to the scene, and the overall aesthetics are guided by a visionary creative director. These efforts come together to produce visuals that bid readers to escape into our dreamy milieu.

While perusing this book or the magazine, images can be interpreted as both aspirational and inspirational. In some circumstances, a photo may illuminate a path that can be followed to perfection. Perhaps within these pages, for example, you will discover a china pattern that prompts a new collection, a recipe soon to become your signature dish, or furnishings ideally suited to an upcoming remodeling project. In other cases, the value gleaned may be more general, as you respond to a color palette or overall mood that resonates with your style.

In creating conversation around the theme of welcome, I will share personal observations regarding many past features. Our editorial team presents each story in hopes that the content will benefit readers, whether the impact is directly applicable or more subtle in its influence. As you make your way through this book, I hope that you will find a wealth of practical ideas, wisdom, and encouragement to tuck into your heart.

MAY YOUR HOME RISE UP TO MEET YOU

"A welcoming home is a place of refuge," writes Emilie Barnes in *The Spirit of Loveliness*. "A place where people worn down by the noise and turmoil and hostility of the outside world can find a safe resting place.

A welcoming home is a place that you and others enjoy coming home to." These words speak to the universal longing for a space that at once relaxes and invigorates. However, for many of us—and especially women—in a desire to create an atmosphere of family warmth and hospitality, it can be easy to turn our gazes outward while losing sight of the haven that home can also be to us as individuals.

This was an especially trying balance for me during the early years of child-rearing. I recall one summer when weeks of togetherness and travel had taken their toll on our surroundings. With our family of six home most of the day, staying on top of meal preparation, kitchen cleanup, and laundry often left me with little time to clean the rest of the house. I focused most of my housekeeping on maintaining the more public spaces but soon realized that our primary bedroom was in desperate need of attention. Half-empty suitcases stood against the wall as reminders of recent trips, while toddler toys and shoes scattered the walkway. I set up the ironing board in a corner as a temporary measure, but it remained there for a week.

Soon, I realized how much this neglected bedroom was dimming my joy. Rather than providing a revitalizing retreat, the space actually drained me of energy. Awaking to the sight of my ironing board, my first thoughts were of the mountains of housework awaiting me. And I arose already feeling defeated.

So, I set my aim on reclaiming that oasis. After emptying the room of clutter, I vacuumed, dusted, and tidied every surface. Invigorated by the newly restored sense of order, my thoughts turned to the yards of fabric tucked beneath the bed. In college, I fashioned window treatments out of sheets and pillowcases. I played with fabric—looping, pleating, and fluffing it until it looked just right—then tucking under any unfinished edges. But when we bought a proper house, somehow, I felt the rules had changed. I dutifully lined my curtains, sewed pretty trims on pillows, and approached every home-improvement project with the utmost dedication. I had intended

to make a canopy for the four-poster bed, but I never could seem to find the time to make all the panels I would need. Eventually, I pushed that pretty pink chintz under the bed, and there it sat for more than five years.

When I finally gave myself permission to let go of perfectionism, I brought the fabric out and played with it. I unfurled, draped, gathered, and cut it. As I allowed the floral print to puddle gracefully onto the floor and smoothed the edges, I smiled, realizing I had created the place of refuge my restless heart had been yearning for.

In times of busyness, and particularly during seasons of caretaking, life may require a level of sacrifice that feels nearly complete in its demands. This pouring out of self can be a mission of holy purpose and one that holds the potential to shape the giver into a more mature, grounded, and compassionate person. However, devotion can turn to depletion if the vessel is continually emptied but never replenished. Anne Morrow Lindbergh laments in *Gift from the Sea*, "Eternally, woman spills herself away in driblets to the thirsty, seldom being allowed the time, the quiet, the peace, to let the pitcher fill up to the brim."

Considering aspects of one's being that require consistent sustenance, efforts to nurture mind, body, and spirit might feel vain or unnecessary but remain vital for overall health and happiness. Amid the whir of everyday life, carving out time for reading, fellowship, exercise, and prayer can be difficult, but these pursuits hold reservoirs of joy and peace. Just as

ACTS OF LOVELINESS

Consider these suggestions for cultivating a spirit of welcome that enriches your daily life.

• Address areas that greet you upon entering your home, first clearing away any clutter and then arranging vignettes that will delight your eye each time you open the door.

• Even when dining alone, choose pretty plates and flatware, appreciating the glimmers of beauty these special pieces add to your meal.

• Display framed prints of favorite scriptures or quotes to remind yourself of wise and encouraging words.

• Sleep on the finest bedding that your budget allows. And if your nicest sheets are hidden away in a cupboard for safekeeping, realize that most household textiles actually fare better with regular use and laundering.

• Assess the scene that awaits when you open your eyes each morning. Would repositioning the bed afford a clearer view of the world outside your window?

• As often as possible, snip a few blooms to create a fragrant posy for your bedside table, desk, or bathroom counter.

• Develop routines that ease you into and out of the day. The benefits of a cup of tea in the morning and a stroll through the neighborhood at sunset can last from dawn to dusk.

nutritious foods fuel body and mind, allowing peak performance, a nourishing environment refreshes both physically and emotionally, ultimately enhancing service to others.

When I set out to create a boudoir, I worried that this endeavor might push the rest of my family out of the space, but instead I found that the softness and tranquility drew them in. Our whole family shared story time, snuggle time, and devotional time under that canopy of dreams. And each morning I awoke, ready to venture out from my haven, eager to embrace the imperfect beauty beyond my bedroom doors.

DESIGNED FOR THE ENJOYMENT OF ALL

Banks of 'Limelight' hydrangeas, with their profusion of enormous chartreuse blooms, roll out a vibrant welcome to the Georgia home of Marsha Mason. Brimful annual and perennial beds envelop her 1926 Tudor charmer—its visage softened by verdant tendrils of creeping fig clambering up the façade and a canopy of fragrant 'New Dawn' roses that stretches over the front porch. Window boxes spilling over with lemon cypress, 'Macho' fern, and ivy invite a peek inside, where sun-washed quarters convey the same exuberance as the lush surroundings.

Surveying Marsha's house and gardens, it is difficult to believe that this vision of seasonal splendor ever languished. But when the Masons discovered the cottage in 2001, the interior decorator recalls that it was in terrible condition. "From the street, it looked like

a big brick rectangle with no curb appeal," she says. "I only had the courage to show one friend. I kept everyone else away until it was renovated."

On the day of purchase, every living room window was hidden behind shutters, sheers, and curtains. "The first thing I did," she says, "was pull it all down." Over nine months, the family worked within the dwelling's original footprint to reconfigure an awkward layout. With a better flow established, Marsha was able to flood dark, dreary corners with natural light. She sewed new drapes and coated walls in cheery hues. Furnished with antiques, artwork, and collectibles, revitalized spaces became favorite spots to linger.

In interviewing Marsha for a feature in *Victoria*, I learned that when lending her talents to a project, she recognizes that the dwelling must suit its dwellers. "A space that is not livable serves no purpose, no matter how beautiful it is," she says. The designer considers carefully how each room will function—factoring in clients' stage of life and way of life—to satisfy unique priorities. In her own quarters, where hospitality is prized, slipcovers give a polished appearance to Chippendale chairs but allow for easy cleaning. She recommends carrying out this idea in washable fabrics with dressmaker details, such as covered-button closures.

A devoted grandmother of six, Marsha today fields as many questions on developing "kid-friendly" areas as she did when her daughters and son were small. "Long gone are the days of roping off the living room and dining room because they are too precious to use," she says. Accommodating children, though, does not mean removing breakables from every surface. Instead, she suggests exposing little ones to beautiful things while teaching

As displayed in the home of Marsha Mason, thoughtful design choices help a home extend a welcome to all who inhabit the space, whether this encompasses a menagerie of pets or multiple generations of family. Choices abound for tailoring a space to the unique needs of its residents, including a range of performance fabrics, comfortably proportioned furniture pieces, and a variety of flooring options.

respect for their fragility. "The added bonus," she points out, "is that you'll never need to worry about their behavior in someone else's home."

For this interior designer, color remains an enduring inspiration. Although she can appreciate the serenity of a neutral palette, in her own environs, Marsha finds joy among vivid yellows, greens, and blues punctuated with bright accents of coral or salmon. "No matter where I travel, I am always happy to come home to my little cottage," she says. "I hope it is as welcoming to others as it is to me."

LEARNING THEIR LANGUAGES

Several years ago, while navigating the full calendar of an active family, I asked my adolescent children to contemplate this question: What one thing makes you feel most welcome in our home? With all four involved in extracurricular interests on top of our commitments to church, school, and work, we experienced some of our busiest yet most memorable days during that season of opportunity.

Amid overlapping activities, I often reflected on these sentiments from Harriet Beecher Stowe: "Home is a place not only of strong affections, but of entire unreserve; it is life's undress rehearsal, its backroom, its dressing room." Think of the comfort of crossing the threshold of this haven as evening falls. With grateful sighs, we relax our shoulders as we shed backpacks and briefcases, ballet shoes and soccer cleats, as well as the load of any stresses or worries we may have carried throughout the day. Especially when so much living takes place beyond the doors of your house, home can and should remain a cherished oasis.

Phrases such as "progress over perfection" were a frequent refrain during that stage, as tasks of cooking and homekeeping sometimes slipped through the cracks of a packed schedule. In determining goals, I wanted to know what each member of the family valued most about our life together.

This would allow us to release some expectations while holding fast to those deemed most important.

To introduce the topic, I told everyone that I appreciate coming home at night to find that someone has turned on the porch light. This is not a gesture that my husband or children necessarily notice, but I interpret that golden glow as a message that someone is waiting eagerly for my return when I am away after dark. My older son said that he feels cared for if we have cereal stocked in the pantry, while one of my daughters mentioned playing board games as her favorite shared pastime. These and other simple suggestions allowed us to speak graciously to one another through a series of courtesies and kindnesses.

Sometimes, we cannot accomplish everything on our to-do lists, but most of the time we can do the one thing that means the most. It is worth determining, for ourselves, what that priority would be. And it is also enlightening to ask the question of those closest to us.

This conversation is one that I hope our family will continue to explore. As I write this volume, I am adjusting to my new role as a "bird launcher." What a joy it is to watch them soar! Of course, I look forward to having my children back in the nest, and those reunions will always be my happiest days. Whenever one of them can fly home, you can be sure that I will be prepared with homemade pie, freshly washed sheets, or a puzzle ready for completion. And as our family grows to include other special friends, spouses, and—one day, when the time is right—precious babies of their own, I hope to become even more fluent in the language of welcome that speaks to each and every heart.

"If you slow down and take pleasure in simple things, you are more likely to lead a contented and well-balanced existence."

—Jennifer L. Scott

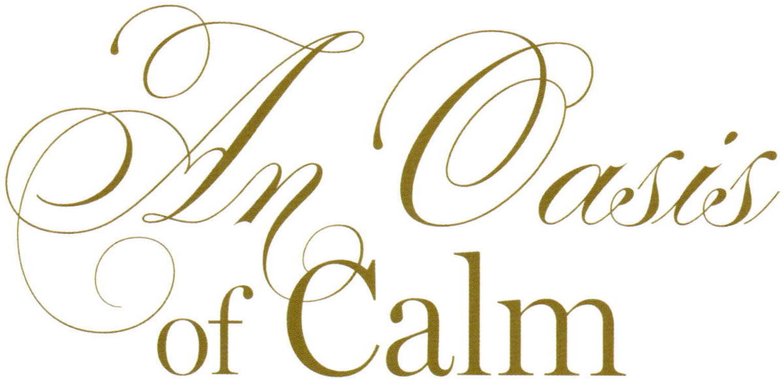

The quiet of early morning finds Sharon Santoni taking in the wonders of her surroundings in France. The calendar promises an excursion to Paris—an easy distance from her home in Normandy—but even the City of Light cannot compete with the natural gifts to be savored within this pastoral oasis. Cup of tea in hand, she surveys cascades of roses, tangles of nigella, and clusters of foxgloves while her dogs frolic nearby.

"As soon as I saw this house, it felt just right," Sharon says. "We are on the edge of a small village, and my children grew up riding in the forest, canoeing on the river, and hosting many a great party in the garden." Built in the late 1850s, the classical *maison de maître* features the symmetrical design and comfortable footprint for which this style of architecture is known. Thick stone walls keep the interiors warm in the winter and cool in the summer. And during temperate weather, the boundaries between house and garden blur as fragrant breezes waft in through doors and windows flung open to invite fresh air.

"While I am fully living a French life," says the British-born author, "I can still see French living from an objective point of view." A sense of élan surrounds the Gallic sensibility, especially when it comes to cultivating a welcoming ambience. The hours seem to unfurl gently here, with tasks of homekeeping establishing a soothing cadence for the day.

"I LOVE THE QUALITY OF OUR EVERYDAY LIFE HERE—THE ATTENTION TO DETAIL, THE BEAUTIFUL ARCHITECTURE AND COUNTRYSIDE."

—Sharon Santoni

Antique textiles abound in France, and Sharon has amassed an enviable cache that she puts to use daily. "Pure linen sheets are smooth and heavy—wonderful to sleep on," she says. "It's true that they need more care than modern sheets, and it's preferable to hang them out to dry, but the effort is worthwhile." Savoring the sun-kissed softness of these timeless European treasures is an everyday pleasure that never loses its allure.

Freshly clipped blooms grace her table, which is laden with flavorful fare. "We really only eat food that is in season in our part of the world," Sharon says. "Food tastes so much better when it's bought locally and has been allowed to ripen without being forced." Fruits and salads brighten menus from spring to early autumn, while leeks and spinach lend coziness to winter meals. During summertime, Sharon often serves chilled strawberry or raspberry parfaits. In petite glass bowls or slender Champagne flutes, she layers sweetened, puréed fruit with ribbons of yogurt or mascarpone and cream. Chopped meringues add pleasing texture to the tiered dessert, while a whole cookie offers the crowning touch to this party favorite.

The most treasured hours of Sharon's day unfold in the tranquil setting of her property. "My garden is an essential part of my life," she says. No matter what adventures the afternoon may bring, she looks forward to returning to this haven in the evening. And when stars twinkle overhead, Sharon retires to her boudoir, where the gentle *ouh ouh* of owls in the garden lulls her to sweet dreams of bliss.

THE CARE AND KEEPING OF LINENS

Properly laundered and stored, linens can serve a lifetime and beyond. Delicate fabrics and precious heirlooms are best surrendered to textile professionals, but most linens can be tended at home. Here are suggestions for maintaining the health of most household textiles.

• Frequent use extends the life of fabrics, so don't keep fine sheets and favorite table linens in reserve for fear that service will diminish their quality. Most textiles fare better when used and laundered regularly, so let them breathe and enjoy the beauty they add to daily life.

• A gracious hostess need not fret when spills soil her table linens. Without a lapse in conversation, she can quickly dab the stain with a cold, wet cloth; rub a sprinkling of table salt over the spot; and cover the blemish with a napkin to avoid further disturbance to the meal. After a dinner party, all table linens need to soak in an ice-water bath for a few hours or even overnight. Stains that do not come out in the bath can be further treated with a stain-removing formula before being washed.

• For fragile fabrics and table linens with delicate handwork or trim, hand washing in the sink with warm water and a mild detergent formulated for textiles is the safest option. Sturdier linens can withstand the tumble of a washing machine on the gentle cycle. Oxygenated bleach is safe for most textiles, but chlorine bleach is not recommended. Handle wet articles with care, squeezing excess water out without twisting or wringing the fabric. Allow vintage or fragile linens to air dry.

• Wash sheets weekly in warm water, turning patterned pillowcases inside out to keep colors vibrant. Freshly pressed sheets feel luxuriously new again, but many fabric blends feel supple and inviting pulled straight from the dryer. Launder mattress covers, pillow protectors, and comforters monthly. Fluff pillows daily, and wash them, two at a time, at least twice a year. Pillows and comforters can last many years with proper care but should be replaced when the fabric starts to fray or the filling loses its loft.

• Crisp linens add polish to a home, but care should be taken in ironing. For best results, lay a terry cloth towel over the ironing board and press damp linens with a dry iron. Delicate cloth should be sandwiched between the towel and a press cloth. If you are unsure how the fabric will handle heat, begin with the iron on the lowest setting and test a small, inconspicuous area before increasing the heat. Keep a spray bottle of distilled water nearby, and spritz as needed to add moisture. Iron embroidered linens on the wrong side to protect the needlework and display the design to its best effect. Most textile experts do not recommend the use of starch—or suggest only starching before use and laundering—as the carbohydrate can cause stored linens to yellow and attract pests.

• Thoughtful storage prolongs the life of treasured linens. Plastic bins do not allow air to circulate, so choose wire or painted wood shelving lined with acid-free paper or cotton fabric for best results. Rolling is gentler on fibers than folding, so consider wrapping a set of napkins or a collection of tea towels around a cardboard tube to avoid creases. A bundle of chalk tied with ribbon and hung in the linen closet draws moisture, while sprigs of lavender add subtle fragrance.

GIFTS OF TRANQUILITY

In order to stretch its arms wide in welcome, a home must embrace the needs of its inhabitants, not merely relegating the accoutrements of daily tasks to forgotten corners but holding sacred space for the stuff of life. When working within an existing layout, the first step comes in assessing room arrangements, as effective furniture placement aids in carrying out responsibilities. For example, tucking an antique secretary in a quiet area, away from the thrum and traffic of the family room, fosters an atmosphere more suited to study.

Positioning necessities within easy reach becomes the next priority. If devoting time to correspondence is a goal, following through on that intention is much easier when stationery, pens, and stamps nestle together in a cubby or drawer. Pausing to write a letter in such a spot can become an oft-enjoyed simple pleasure, thanks to the ease of seeing the idea through to completion.

Applying a fresh perspective may result in creative uses for older pieces that no longer serve their original purpose. Inherited from my husband's family, a wooden case good that functioned for the previous generation as a stereo cabinet now takes pride of place as a buffet. With glass inserts replacing the fabric panels that once disguised speakers, new shelves allow for the display of collected treasures. Similarly, when the proportions of our dining room could not accommodate a weathered china cabinet, the primary bedroom offered the ideal quarters. Coated in creamy white paint and lined with colorful wallpaper saved from a *Victoria* photo shoot, the breakfront showcases a mix of photos, books, and mementos alongside traditional wares, including an Amore by Sadek tea set and our cache of Fostoria sherbet glasses.

Establishing rhythms for cleaning and home maintenance contributes to the overall peacefulness of an environment. "A welcoming home has a sense of order about it," Emilie Barnes explains in *The Spirit of Loveliness*. "Not stiff, stultifying order that goes to pieces over a speck of dust or that sacrifices relationships in the interest of cleanliness, but a comforting, confident sense that life is under control."

With her organized approach to homemaking a balance to my own creative tendencies, my mother set an inspiring example in this regard. Daily, weekly, and seasonal routines ensured that life unfolded within well-tended spaces—a tidiness that not only blessed our family but also ensured that we were nearly always ready for company.

For those, like me, whose minds quickly wander from to-do lists of housekeeping duties to wish lists of imaginative projects, focusing an eye for creativity to mundane tasks can lend sweetness to ordinary days. This yearning permeates former Writer-in-Residence Alexandra Stoddard's classic *Creating a Beautiful Home*. "The way the light falls on my desk in the morning matters terribly to me," she writes. "I do the dishes ... depending on when the light floods into the white porcelain sink, not when the meal is finished." Cleaning the kitchen amid the flicker and fragrance of a candle, folding laundry while listening to an audio book, or sweeping the porch in the mellowing sunshine of golden hour encourages moments of gratitude amid the prosaic details of everyday demands.

After living for twenty-five years amid the symmetry and formality of a Georgian house, interior designer Mary Finch finds comfort amid the more casual environs of a 1920s French Provincial home. "My kitchen feels more like a smaller living space," she says. "I like to turn on the music, open the Dutch door, and watch for my husband to come home from the office."

SENSES & SENSIBILITY

Heighten feelings of serenity by looking beyond the aesthetics of your interiors to consider the entire sensory experience of being in your home.

• Take a few minutes at the end of each day to tidy your surroundings so that you will awake to a welcoming environment. When time does not allow for following through on this suggestion fully, consider the one area that is most important to your sense of well-being and focus your efforts there.

• Whatever your favorite genre, set a tranquil mood with soft strains of music. Slow and simple melodies with gentle harmonies promote relaxation.

• Open your windows during a spring shower not only to reduce humidity and ventilate your home but also to savor the gentle pitter-patter of raindrops, along with the delightfully earthy odor known as *petrichor*.

• To infuse your home with a fragrance known for calming properties, turn to lavender, chamomile, or vanilla.

• Stash a variety of soft blankets in different weights near conversation areas.

• Lend a sweet floral essence to clothing by tucking sachets brimming with potpourri into drawers and closets.

• Fill a pretty bowl with fresh seasonal produce. A bushel of apples adds autumnal color to the kitchen while encouraging a wholesome snack.

• As it circulates the air, let an oscillating fan lull you to sleep with the relaxing sounds of summers past.

• In a glass atomizer, craft a signature fragrance by diluting a few drops of essential oil and a pinch of Epsom salts in distilled water. Spritzing pillows and bedding with the aromatic spray may inspire dreams of the garden.

• If you have a fireplace, set a table before the hearth for the coziest wintertime dinners.

• Add moisture to the air by simmering redolent ingredients in water or apple juice and refreshing the liquid, as needed, throughout the day. Consider citrus slices, fresh herbs, and spices for the medley.

• Savor the sensory experience of making a pot of coffee—listening to it percolate, inhaling the brew's slightly nutty aroma, taking that first bracing sip, and tasting its fresh-roasted flavor.

"I am going to make everything around me beautiful—that will be my life."

—Elsie de Wolfe

Enclaves of Beauty

One evening, while enjoying dinner out when our children were small, my oldest son noticed the prettiest girl in his kindergarten class eating at a nearby table. Determined to say hello, he began walking toward the family but stopped in his tracks a few feet away, unable to speak. Sensing his brother's anxiety and eager to help, 3-year-old Christian called from across the crowded restaurant, "Carson, ask her what her favorite color is!"

From proclaiming our earliest choice of a signature hue to putting the finishing touches on a dream house, defining one's decorating style is a journey of self-discovery that can last a lifetime. Where we feel paralyzed with indecision or fear making a misstep, publications such as *Victoria* share gentle guidance to propel us forward.

The magazine offers endless inspiration to the romantic heart, due in large part to the gracious homeowners who open their doors to our editorial team, allowing us to showcase interiors and tell the stories behind these treasured spaces. From cottage to estate, casual to formal interiors, and muted to bold palette, there is beauty to be discovered at every turn.

In the pages that follow, explore a variety of richly layered rooms brought to life by impassioned creatives. Within these lovely environs, I hope you will find a wealth of ideas for adorning the most precious place of all: the one you call home.

The daughter of an antiques dealer and decorator, Janie Willis honed her eye for heirloom finds during childhood while exploring European markets with her mother. Now a designer in her own right, Janie fills her home with treasured pieces from around the world, including an Italian gilt mirror, French chairs, and English Imari porcelain.

"I BELIEVE PASSIONATELY THAT EVERY WOMAN HAS THE POTENTIAL TO BE A CREATIVE FORCE IN HER SPHERE AND SHOULD FEEL EQUIPPED TO BE THE STYLIST OF HER OWN HOME."

—Jenny Bohannon

At Tallwood, the Virginia estate of former Artist-in-Residence Jenny Bohannon, gracious traditions of the past inspire the homemaker's approach to creating a welcoming milieu for her family and the many guests who visit. Among the icons she looks to for inspiration, Jenny credits revered tastemakers Jackie Kennedy and Bunny Mellon as enduring influences.

The attention to detail that characterizes the exquisite work of jewelry designer Nicola Bathie McLaughlin also informs the look of her interiors. The entrepreneur, who describes herself as "a traditionalist and old soul at heart," showcases cherished Wedgwood and Rose Medallion collections—accessories that add the final grace notes to well-dressed vignettes.

PICASSO
GRAFF

In Nicola's petal-strewn bedroom, freshly clipped blooms echo the florals found in upholstery fabric, bedding, and a pair of framed prints. A demure palette establishes a restful ambience, and favorite volumes bid the busy mother to pause for moments of repose.

“We set out to build a French-European country house that looks like it could have been there a long time,” says Tina Yaraghi, the woman behind The Enchanted Home shop and blog. Realizing this dream, her family’s former New York home evokes images of *maisons* in the Loire Valley.

Faudree Interiors

"I LOVE THE WAY NATURAL LIGHT FLOODS INTO THESE ROOMS AND MAKES THEM BEAUTIFUL FROM THE MOMENT THE SUN RISES UNTIL SUNSET—AND WELL AFTER!" —Tina Yaraghi

SUZANNE KASLER
DECORATING IN DETAIL

Courtney Davey, the creative behind interior design blog and Instagram account Tuft & Trim, looks to her beloved grandmother as the ultimate example of gracious living.

Complementing Courtney's love of beauty is a desire to create functional spaces that meet the needs of her young children—a balance that presents a worthwhile challenge. "Sometimes," she shared in *Victoria* magazine, "fresh paint, tasteful light fixtures, and the right furniture and décor make a world of difference."

Charm School
SUZANNE KASLER TIMELESS STYLE

“When I drive up the mountain, my heart beats faster,” says Ann Monfore, “and when I come through the gates, a peacefulness comes over me.” The reward at the end of this oft-made journey is the welcome of her Victorian-style cottage, where a wide porch bids one to while away the hours relaxing with a cup of tea or catching up with a neighbor who has come to call.

Stone Houses

Within the stately environs of this 1929 stone-clad charmer, also shown on the previous spread, collected treasures tell the story of the couple who abide within these walls. Family heirlooms and restored antiques lend warmth and history to the unfolding of everyday life.

"One cannot help but notice the mesmeric array of fabrics in every area of the house," writer Karen Callaway noted in describing this Virginia abode, which includes a cozy mahogany-paneled library, a dining room wrapped in de Gournay silk wall coverings, and sumptuous conversation areas.

*"Keep good company,
read good books, love good things,
and cultivate soul and
body as faithfully as you can."*

—Louisa May Alcott

Room to Grow

The oasis where we reveal our most vulnerable selves—washing our faces clean of makeup, slipping under the bed covers, closing our eyes, and drifting off to sleep—also provides a haven for our deepest and most heartfelt longings. Home literally gives us the space to dream, both while we slumber and when we awake to pursue the passions and professions that fill our days with meaning. In our abodes, we dare to set goals, develop talents, and nurture progress in an environment of safety and support.

"We live in houses, and when they transcend into homes, they envelop our personality," Alexandra Stoddard attests. "Whatever is right and good about our lives, whatever is authentic and beautiful, will be reflected in the atmosphere as well as in the details that mirror our souls in meaningful, tangible, physical ways."

When our surroundings brim with books, we open new worlds of discovery. Where games and sporting equipment abound, we extend an invitation to play. When a basket of yarn rests beside the hearth, an easel nestles at the window, or fabric fills a sewing room, creativity blossoms. And where a garden flourishes, so does joy.

THE READING LIFE

My father gave me a childhood I treasure. As a girl, I was deaf and blind. Restless and wild, I lived in silence until a teacher named Annie Sullivan spelled W-A-T-E-R and brought the world to the palm of my hand. I lived in a little house with Ma and Pa. My name was Mary, and my sisters were Laura and Carrie. Growing up on the prairie, I knew that Laura and Almanzo would be together forever. As for me, I was waiting for my prince. My stepmother tried to keep me from true love, but I went to the ball, the glass slipper fit, and we lived happily ever after.

My childhood was filled with adventure, mystery, and romance, all because Daddy taught me to lose myself—and find myself—in books. I come from a long line of readers. A librarian for many years, my maternal grandmother felt at home among the stacks. My late grandfather was a

RACING CALENDAR
1843

"THE LOVE OF LEARNING,
THE SEQUESTERED NOOKS,
AND ALL THE SWEET SERENITY OF BOOKS."

—Henry Wadsworth Longfellow

college professor who filled journals with notes from his studies. When my grandmother remarried a book lover later in life, volumes had so overtaken this bachelor's home that she had to remove them from the stove and bathtub to set up housekeeping.

If I was a bookworm by nature, my upbringing provided the nurture. Story time was a nighttime ritual I relished as a little girl. With funny voices and sound effects, Daddy breathed life into the tales he read. Together, we cheered *The Little Engine That Could* to keep trying, shook our heads at the antics of Curious George, and yawned sleepily when the time came to say *Good Night, Little Bear*.

My father believed you could never spoil a child with books, and my favorite present under the Christmas tree often turned out to be the one he chose just for me. I can recall many times when I stayed up late after the holiday, so enthralled with a new title that I had to read just one more page, one more chapter, before I could turn out the light. Books are also the perfect gift for my dad. A shirt and tie are received with polite appreciation, but a new read makes his eyes light up. His personal library has surpassed five thousand volumes, but he can always make room for one more.

I am so thankful that my heritage taught me to love reading. My father showed me that the best place to find yourself—in life and in books—is somewhere between "once upon a time" and "the end," because that is where the magic happens. And when you are a reader, you approach each day with anticipation, eager to see what the next chapter brings.

LET'S PLAY

• Dedicate a cabinet in your family's gathering area to board games. A nearby drawer can hold playing cards and dominoes.

• Pay tribute to a child's favorite athletic pursuit in his or her bedroom. For a son or daughter who loves rugby or soccer, for example, create a colorful display of framed jerseys.

• Over a holiday break or when hosting loved ones for several days, encourage unhurried hours of bliss with a puzzle. Scattered across a spare table, the pieces invite togetherness as guests wander by and can't resist lending a hand.

• If tennis or badminton are endeavors of choice, stash rackets in an umbrella stand in the foyer or hang them from hooks in a mudroom.

• Antique sporting equipment can make for charming décor in a family room or den.

• If space and interest allow, a billiard table can provide hours of enjoyment.

• Let love of the game inspire your entertaining, as suggested by this croquet party featured in *Victoria*. This summer social unfolds on carpets of grass dappled in golden sunlight.

"PLAY IS THE ROYAL ROAD TO CHILDHOOD HAPPINESS AND ADULT BRILLIANCE."
—Joseph Chilton Pearce

MLP

ENCOURAGING ARTISTIC EXPRESSION

Visiting the homes of beloved matriarchs opened my heart to the blessings of creativity. My paternal grandmother, a gifted musician whose fingers glided daily over the keys of her piano, also used her hands to paint, crochet, and craft. While she preferred quick sewing patterns—garments, costumes, and small quilts that she could turn out in an afternoon—my maternal grandmother invested her hours into fewer but more intricate projects. I marvel at the delicate motifs adorning tablecloths she cross-stitched over many months and remember the sublime pleasure of twirling in a new dress or skirt she had carefully constructed.

Like the amazing women in my family, artisans we feature in the magazine discover wellsprings of contentment in devoting hours to honing their gifts. Gracing these pages are the works of three such creatives, with linens embroidered by Viley Nelson shown on the opposite page, a trio of rosy canvases brought to life by Carolina Elizabeth on page 86, and a gallery wall of oil paintings by Kristie Shelton on page 87. These inspiring figures have developed their talents into businesses of bliss.

Whether efforts unfurl in a quiet corner or an airy workshop, focusing energy into producing beauty brings a unique satisfaction. Throughout life, as we explore different avenues of creativity and find that an interest blossoms into a passion, our homes can grow with us in shifting to provide space for a new dream.

My maternal grandfather often remarked that he loved listening to my grandmother's sewing machine—a promising whir that rang out from an alcove of their cozy den. My heart feels the same sense of delight today when my daughter Mary Ashley retreats to her attic studio to sew, and I hear the hopeful rumble of imagination taking flight.

In considering creative talent, which can be described as artistic aptitude, I have always believed that interests may reveal pools of talent that are as yet unexplored. For the painter, musician, or sewist, there was a first time to pick up the paintbrush, instrument, or needle. Continuing to expand our skills throughout life may lead to the discovery of new gifts.

AMONG THE BLOSSOMS

Of the many landscapes showcased in *Victoria* over the past decade, the setting of a century-old farmhouse in Prince Edward Island remains an enduring favorite. Carolyn Aiken tends this idyllic site, coaxing lilacs, delphiniums, daylilies, and more to bloom on the 10-acre property where she raised seven children amid cooling Canadian breezes and the ripples of a babbling brook. Husband Andrew lent his carpentry skills to the scene, building arbors, fences, and a charming garden shed.

Although I lack the passion and expertise that lead many of our readers to nurture such halcyon surroundings, there are few activities I enjoy more than arranging cut flowers. When hosting a luncheon or tea party, I take great delight in creating a centerpiece for the table. The floral bounty not only adds beauty to the occasion but continues to delight for days following the event—a lovely reminder of times shared. Hydrangeas, roses, and tulips are often my stems of choice, but the happiest day is discovering that ruffly pink peonies are in season once again.

Whether cultivating an outdoor sanctuary or slipping a posy onto the nightstand, such amusements connect us to nature. The simple act of gathering budding spring branches into a tall vase, adding cascades of colorful pumpkins to porch steps, or piling lemons into a blue-and-white porcelain bowl encourages us to inhale deeply the sweet and ephemeral breath of life.

"I LOVE BEING OUT HERE SURROUNDED BY BEAUTY AND ALL THE SIGHTS, SOUNDS, AND FRAGRANCES OF NATURE."

—Carolyn Aiken

Where efforts are invested into cultivating an outdoor oasis, consider also creating a haven for relaxing among the blooms. Carolyn Aiken's property offers well-placed seating areas where one can enjoy refreshment, whether in the form of a quiet breeze or an amiable conversation.

"In the circle of the hearth everything is good, but reminiscences are best of all."

—Elisabeth Woodbridge Morris

Haven of Memories

Penning these words over a holiday weekend, I wait expectantly for daughter Emma, coming in from her freshman year of college to savor the final moments of summer with a visit to her grandparents. At the lakeside home of my in-laws, sunlight shimmers on the water like a rippling cache of blue sapphires, the traditional gift representing the sixty-fifth wedding anniversary they celebrate this week. A boat glides quietly through the swells as a heron makes its graceful arc overhead.

The Lesters' Georgian-style abode, built in 1950 by Atlanta architectural firm Ivey and Crook, whispers the tales of a long and faithful marriage. Antiques and artwork collected during their travels mingle with handmade treasures, such as colorful bargello seat covers featuring embroidery wool my mother-in-law purchased decades ago on a trip to the Scottish Highlands. Shelves brim with yearbooks, trophies, and family photos—mementos of the three children raised within these walls.

Adding to the comfort of returning to this place are traditions celebrated among kith and kin. "In its own way, a ritual is a form of time-magic," former Writer-in-Residence Erica Bauermeister explains. "It takes the endless flow of life and slows it down long enough for us to pay attention, to put the stamp of our experience on an otherwise ephemeral moment." During times of transition, such as adjusting to life at a large university, there is such sweet solace in the assurance of being welcomed with simple

gifts: a breakfast of pancakes and bacon, afternoons spent splashing in the water, evenings passed playing dominoes. Like a dish of pound cake topped with vanilla ice cream and fresh peaches, familiar pleasures are often the most sublime—especially when they are shared with loved ones who have come to call. "Rituals create mental rooms in our minds where those moments can live," Erica adds, "and in doing so, give them meaning. Help us remember."

Within the sacred shelter of constancy, generations meet. Memories of the past echo in stories of the great-grandparents who originally lived in this house but moved a few doors down to make way for their son's growing family. Easing his pontoon boat into the dock after giving us a tour of the lake, my father-in-law recalls tender moments between his parents. "Every afternoon after work, Big Daddy would take Nanelle out for a boat ride," he says wistfully. Emma listens closely, dreaming of days to come, as across the sapphire deep, the heron settles into its nest.

PRESERVING THE PAST

Let these ideas from *Victoria* help you chronicle your family's unfolding story.

• To recall favorite eateries where she has dined with her husband, interior designer Kathryn Greeley displays a gallery of restaurant menus in the kitchen of her beloved abode, Chestnut Cottage.

• During a trip to Scotland on behalf of the magazine, Creative Director of Lifestyle Melissa Sturdivant Smith brought back a single autumn leaf, which she matted in a pretty frame etched with the country and date.

• In the mountain bungalow of former Writer-in-Residence Jan Karon, bowls brim with a brilliant miscellany of reminiscences—roses delivered by a friend, petals saved from a corsage, stems gathered during garden strolls. "Hardly a flower comes into this house that I can bear to part with," says the author. Long after their life in the vase, fresh-cut bouquets continue to add beauty, transformed by her hands into colorful potpourri.

• "As an antiques dealer, I am always trying to incorporate heirlooms into our home's design in new ways," says Lidy Barrs of FrenchGardenHouse. She finds creative uses for Gallic finds, such as using an enamelware canister to showcase bundles of cutlery on a buffet or creating a floral arrangement in an ironstone pitcher.

TREASURES TO SIP AND SAVOR

"Tea is quiet," explains author and tea authority James Norwood Pratt, "and our thirst for tea is never far from our craving for beauty." Many of my loveliest moments have unfolded over teatime—beginning my day in the hush of early morning with a steaming brew, welcoming friends to my table for an afternoon of conversation and dainty treats, or traveling to an exotic destination and taking tea in the elegant environs of a historic venue. Whether a few minutes of solitude or leisurely hours shared in the company of loved ones, teatime, for me, is always an occasion to be sipped and savored.

In my home, accoutrements related to serving tea have been given pride of place. Many of these treasures were purchased during visits to tearooms, and their presence evokes fond memories. A porcelain teacup and saucer, tucked among cookbooks in the kitchen, bring back memories of the sweet friend who first invited me to tea and then gifted me afterward with this rose-covered memento. A trio of white cake plates highlights a buffet in our living room—their shapely pedestals and gently scalloped edges an artful complement to the serene décor. And gleaming atop a tufted ottoman in the sitting room, a silver tray showcases a selection of my favorite teapots.

These teapots, in particular, hold a special place in my heart. When my husband was in law school and we lived frugally on my meager salary, going to tea felt like an ultimate luxury. Joe does not share my affinity for much of the traditional tea menu, but he loved watching my eyes light up at the sight of such exquisite offerings. During those years, we celebrated my December birthday with an annual visit to an area tearoom, and after our meal, I would wait eagerly in the car while he purchased my Christmas present from items I had pointed out in the gift shop. Decades later, I appreciate not only the prettiness of these keepsakes but also the sacrifice of love that each one represents.

Today, these teapots add a grace note to my interiors. Sometimes they catch my eye on a busy day, stirring sentimental thoughts of the past. Other days, they encourage me to slow down, brew a fresh pot of a seasonal blend, and fill our prettiest china cups for an impromptu teatime. For parties, they often crown the table, brimming with fragrant blossoms. Always, they give me glimpses of beauty and remind me how truly blessed I am.

THROUGH THE SEASONS

Just as home is both the place where we showcase our memories and the site where so many of those precious moments unfold, this haven reflects the beauty of the shifting calendar while welcoming the blessings brought by every stage of life. As a favorite scripture reminds me, "To every thing there is a season, and a time to every purpose under the heaven."

Spring beckons like a rich green carpet that has been pulled from storage, shaken of its icy crystals, and unfurled over hill and dale. Draped in a profusion of blossoms, this verdant beginning brings to mind the early years of independence, when obtaining an education and establishing home and career become priorities. Summer finds the garden reaching its peak of splendor and sunshine stretching as far as the eye can imagine. This golden era brings the fullness of long days spent cultivating talents, tending responsibilities, and growing a family. With the crunch of leaves under tawny boots, the path leads into autumn, with the rewards of a brilliant harvest reaped personally and professionally. Soon enough, winter arrives, bringing stillness and quiet to the glowing hearth as snowflakes dance outside the window.

SUCCESS TO TRADE
AND BILLS WELL PAID

"FLOWERS PLAY A KEY ROLE IN BRINGING A SORT OF YOUTHFUL ELEGANCE AND ROMANCE TO TALLWOOD'S INTERIORS AND TABLES AS SPRING ARRIVES." —Jenny Bohannon

The Victorian farmhouse of Kelli Delaney Kot brings to mind sentiments from Celia Thaxter: "There will be eternal summer in the grateful heart." At Maple Shade, double Dutch doors open to views of lush gardens abloom with hydrangeas, roses, delphinium, and lavender.

"I THINK THAT EVERY HOUSE HAS A SEASON, AND PANTRY HILL'S IS AUTUMN."

—Darien Rozell

Bidding the homeowner to ease into the morning with a few cherished moments of quiet, winter comforts abound within this tranquil bedroom: a silver tray laden with the makings of tea for one, an array of plush pillows, and an extra blanket to guard against a chill.

"The ornament of a house is the friends who frequent it."

—Ralph Waldo Emerson

Dwelling with Bonhomie

When home is a place of belonging that nurtures the spirits of all who inhabit the space, flinging wide the doors of that abode becomes a natural extension of its gracious purpose. Inviting guests to step into the rhythms of daily life, walking alongside the family for a time, sets the scene for creating lasting memories.

Welcoming overnight company, especially, encourages a shared vulnerability between host and guest. For the homeowner, the impending arrival of visitors often serves as motivation for completing a litany of tasks. This much-needed boost can prove helpful in taking care of neglected chores, polishing interiors, and laying a mantle of serenity. However, it is easy to let insecurities dim the joy of expecting callers. A room furnished with castaway finds, the window needing repair, a persnickety appliance that requires coaxing to work—the little quirks and flaws that residents live with day to day can seem glaringly apparent and so much more significant under the gaze of someone new. On the other end, the guest may feel unsure of household routines and concerned with the possibility of imposing. However, where both sides may expect to experience judgment, the more likely discovery is acceptance.

The reward for this mutual openness and authenticity is a deepening of relationships. The best hostess is simply a friend: someone who is willing to give of her life and time. In sharing her heart, she finds that many strangers

are actually kindred spirits. Longtime friends whose paths have diverged treasure the opportunity to reconnect, picking up again during a weekend stay as if no time has passed. And familial bonds grow stronger, with brothers, sisters, or other relatives revisiting precious moments from their collective pasts.

There is such sweet joy in conversations that continue into the wee hours, long after the candles have burned down. A passage in *Victoria* Classics Book Club selection *Gift from the Sea* lingers in my thoughts. Anne Morrow Lindbergh writes, "This is what one thirsts for, I realize, after the smallness of the day, of work, of details, of intimacy—even of communication, one thirsts for the magnitude and universality of a night full of stars, pouring into one like a fresh tide."

There is something so peaceful about daylight fading to darkness. Taking in the wonders of a vast inky sky sprinkled with diamonds, host and guest find in companionship the refreshment the author craves: "We walk up the beach under the stars. We feel stretched, expanded to take in their compass. They pour into us until we are filled with stars, up to the brim."

Bread
Box

PLANNING FOR THE COMFORT OF GUESTS

When I consider the heart of hospitality, I reflect on the exuberant greeting I received in visiting the homes of my grandparents. My parents were high school sweethearts, so returning to their hometown afforded time with both families.

There are so few people in the world who fall in love with the very idea of you, wait expectantly for your arrival, mark the day of your birth as one of the best of their lives, and cherish every detail of seeing your face for the first time. This unbridled affection only grows through the years. "Nobody can do for little children what grandparents do," writes Alex Haley. "Grandparents sort of sprinkle stardust over the lives of little children."

In my mind, a grandmother's embrace offers the perfect image of welcome. Time seems to slow in the presence of this matriarch, allowing a gentle unfolding of hours spent with her. There is always room for you at her table, which offers signature dishes perfected over decades. For the moment, your favorite pastimes are hers too, whether your inclinations lean toward academic, artistic, or athletic pursuits. Over many reunions, seeing her eyes light up at the sight of you allows you to bask in a special sunshine that continues to warm your heart long after she is gone.

Looking to sleepovers at the home of grandparents, what makes those stays so special is not the magnificence of the interiors or an elaborate itinerary. The value comes in being truly and wholly enveloped by love. This example provides inspiration for attending to guests. Being keenly attuned to their needs allows us to see to their comfort—draping an extra blanket over a chair, placing a carafe of cool water on the bedside table, ensuring easy access to electrical outlets, or placing a selection of toiletries in the bathroom. When our attitudes communicate joy, these acts of service leave an indelible impression.

MOMENTS OF PAMPERING

Add a thoughtful touch to the guest bath by making a simple but nourishing mixture that visitors can use each time they wash their hands.

HOMEMADE SUGAR SCRUB

Makes approximately ¾ cup

¾ cup granulated sugar
½ cup extra-virgin olive oil
1 tablespoon lemon juice (freshly squeezed or bottled)

In a small mixing bowl, stir together sugar, olive oil, and lemon juice. Transfer mixture to a small jar, sugar bowl, or candy dish. Keep sugar scrub at room temperature. To use, gently rub a spoonful of mixture over hands to exfoliate. Rinse with warm water and pat skin dry.

WHISPERS OF SEA AND SKY

When friends come to call for the weekend, a freshly cut bouquet of blue and white hydrangeas offers an amiable greeting. A tableau arranged with coordinating transferware presents the evening's menu to best effect, while alabaster textiles edged in delicate azure embroidery transform guest quarters into sanctuaries of relaxation.

"No other palette, in its many hues, is as enduring as blue and white," affirms Lexington, Kentucky–based designer Nancy Iliff, noting that the pairing has found favor in many cultures throughout time. Among the many colors featured in her home-décor shop, Linens Limited, the classic combination is a perennial top seller. It is an affinity Nancy shares with her clientele. "My own collection of eighteenth-century English delftware always makes me feel good when I walk into the room," she says. Dutch ceramic tiles frame the fireplace in her abode, and cabinets flanking the hearth showcase an assortment of tin-glazed earthenware objects.

Highlighted in these pages are bedrooms that demonstrate the tranquil effects of the color scheme. The former Columbus, Georgia, home of Ansley Forsberg, whose living room appears on pages 4–5, exudes Colonial Revival charm. While the intensity of the hue varies in different areas of her interiors, the palest tints of blue lend an airy calm to the boudoir showcased in this chapter, with ethereal bedding adding to its sense of restfulness. In Houston, Texas, the bedroom Nicola Bathie McLaughlin designed for her daughters serves as inspiration for dressing guest quarters in a mix of lovely patterns. Crowned with half tester canopies, twin beds invite repose, with the bedside table that is tucked between offering a pair of lamps.

Whether creating a personal haven or extending a sense of welcome to loved ones, adding elements of blue and white lays the foundation for gracious moments not soon to be forgotten. As potter, designer, and author Jonathan Adler explains, "Every blue plays well with every other blue, and the right shade can transport you from the rain-soaked English countryside to the Aegean Sea. It's a miracle color."

"BLUE IS THE ONLY COLOR WHICH MAINTAINS ITS OWN CHARACTER IN ALL ITS TONES."

—Raoul Dufy

KEYS FROM THE INNKEEPER

As sweet as the fruit-filled pies that made this retreat famous, a stay at the quaint and comfortable Berry Manor Inn offers a recipe for relaxation in the heart of Midcoast Maine. A century after the shingle-style Victorian mansion was constructed for a prominent local merchant in the shore village of Rockland, Cheryl Michaelsen and her husband, Michael LaPosta, converted the 1898 residence into a bed-and-breakfast. Their warm-hearted manner of hospitality offers inspiration for homeowners looking to welcome houseguests with signature style.

Richness characterizes the inn's appearance, amenities, and ambience. The interiors have been furnished with antique and reproduction pieces yet are fitted with modern conveniences important to today's travelers. From a multicourse gourmet breakfast served in the dining room each morning to delectable chocolates placed on the pillow every evening, memorable fare abounds throughout each stay.

An atmosphere of approachability envelops patrons, thanks in part to the innkeepers' extended family. More than two decades ago, Cheryl's and Michael's mothers, Ally Taylor and Janet LaPosta, established one of the B&B's most beloved traditions. The pair garnered acclaim for their homemade pies, a penchant for remembering individuals' favorite flavors, and a friendly rivalry over whose crust was best.

In a televised baking competition with Food Network Chef Bobby Flay, Janet offered this simple test for determining a winning dessert: "Would you get up in the night to eat it?" Although the original Pie Moms, as they were dubbed in national media, have since passed their rolling pins to other experienced bakers, their legacy continues with a fully stocked pantry of treats. And success is still measured by the number of guests who return to Berry Manor Inn for a taste of the good life.

THE FRENCH MORNING BREADBASKET

Guests are sure to delight in waking to a luxuriant sampling evocative of the most charming Parisian pâtisserie. Recipes developed in the magazine's test kitchens range from simple indulgences using prepared ingredients to gourmet specialties sure to enchant the experienced baker. Every sumptuous offering, flaky bite, and mouthwatering crumb extends a sublime welcome to the day.

Bring the taste of an authentic Gallic auberge or street-side café to the table with an assortment of treats highlighting a breadth of flavors, from intriguing seasonings and rich chocolate to the freshest fruits of early summer. Raspberry-Nectarine Bostock, as tempting to the eye as to the palate, comes together quickly for an easy yet impressive focal point for the brunch menu. Day-old brioche—brushed with syrup, spread with preserves, and sprinkled with frangipane—becomes a tasty canvas for an array of luscious toppings. For another nearly effortless addition, consider Chaussons Aux Pommes, listed among the most popular breakfast selections in France. Similar to an apple turnover, the *Victoria* recipe wraps luscious filling made from Golden Delicious and Granny Smith varieties in store-bought puff pastry.

For the culinary artist, our chefs present a more ambitious pairing well worth the time and attention involved in creation. Both options feature laminated dough, and impressive results ensure that the making of each recipe will be a rewarding endeavor. Ginger-Cardamom Kouign-Amann showcases tantalizing layers infused with a mixture of sugar and ground spices, cut into squares, and pressed into muffin cups. In the oven's heat, the interior of each serving turns moist and fluffy, while its burnished, ruffly exterior deepens to a crisp caramelized finish. An alternative to the croissant or pain au chocolat, Escargot Au Chocolat boasts decadent whorls of pastry filled with cocoa almond cream. A dusting of confectioners' sugar adds the sweetest of grace notes to these perfect spirals.

RASPBERRY-NECTARINE BOSTOCK

Makes 8

1⅔ cups superfine blanched almond flour
9 tablespoons granulated sugar, divided
¾ teaspoon kosher salt
⅓ cup unsalted butter, cubed and softened
1 large egg, room temperature
¾ teaspoon almond extract
½ teaspoon vanilla bean paste
3 tablespoons water
8 (1-inch) slices day-old brioche (see Note)
2 tablespoons raspberry preserves
2 medium firm ripe nectarines (approximately 10 ounces)
16 ripe fresh raspberries
⅓ cup sliced almonds
1 tablespoon finely chopped raw shelled pistachios
Garnish: confectioners' sugar

1. In the work bowl of a food processor, combine almond flour, 6 tablespoons granulated sugar, and salt; pulse until well combined. Add butter, egg, almond extract, and vanilla bean paste; pulse until smooth and well combined, scraping down sides as needed.

2. Transfer almond mixture to a small bowl; cover and set aside.

3. In a small saucepan, combine 3 tablespoons water and remaining 3 tablespoons granulated sugar; cook over medium heat until sugar dissolves, stirring frequently, 2 to 3 minutes.

4. Preheat oven to 350°. Line a rimmed baking sheet with parchment paper; lightly grease with cooking spray.

5. Brush water mixture liberally on both sides of each bread slice; spread preserves evenly over one side of slices (approximately ¾ teaspoon each).

6. Divide almond mixture evenly among bread slices; spread into an even layer using a small offset spatula.

7. Halve nectarines; remove and discard pits. Cut lengthwise into 24 wedges (each approximately ½- to ¾-inch thick), and thoroughly pat dry with a paper towel; divide and arrange nectarines and raspberries evenly over bread slices. Sprinkle with sliced almonds and pistachios, as desired.

8. Bake for 10 minutes; rotate pan halfway and continue to bake until edges of almond mixture are lightly golden, about 9 minutes more. Let cool on pan for 10 minutes. Serve warm, or let cool to room temperature. Garnish with a dusting of confectioners' sugar before serving, if desired.

Note: Place brioche slices in an even layer on a parchment-lined rimmed baking sheet. Let stand, uncovered, at room temperature overnight.

CHAUSSONS AUX POMMES

Makes 12

Filling:
1 cup (¾- to 1-inch) peeled chopped Golden Delicious apple (approximately 1 large apple)
1 cup (¾- to 1-inch) peeled chopped Granny Smith apple (approximately 1 large apple)
¼ teaspoon orange zest
2 tablespoons fresh orange juice
1½ tablespoons granulated sugar
2 tablespoons assorted raisins
½ teaspoon vanilla extract

Syrup:
3 tablespoons granulated sugar
3 tablespoons water

Pastry:
2 (14-ounce) packages all-butter frozen puff pastry*, thawed according to package directions
2 large egg yolks
1 tablespoon water

1. For filling: In a medium saucepan, combine Golden Delicious and Granny Smith apples, orange zest and juice, and sugar. Bring to a boil over medium-high heat, stirring frequently. Cover and reduce heat to medium-low; cook, stirring often, until apples are softened, 10 to 15 minutes. Remove from heat; using a potato masher or a fork, roughly mash apples. Stir in raisins and vanilla extract; spread apple mixture in a thin layer in a large rimmed baking dish. Let cool completely.
2. For syrup: In a small saucepan, combine sugar and 3 tablespoons water; cook over medium heat, stirring frequently, until sugar is dissolved. Remove from heat; set aside.
3. Preheat oven to 400°. Line 2 rimmed baking sheets with parchment paper.
4. For pastry: Working with one pastry sheet, unroll pastry on a lightly floured surface. Using a 4-inch fluted round cutter, cut out 6 circles. Gently roll and stretch circles into 5.5x3.5-inch ovals. Repeat with remaining pastry sheet. Discard scraps.
5. In a small bowl, whisk together egg yolks and 1 tablespoon water. Brush ovals with egg mixture. Evenly divide apple mixture among pastry ovals. Fold ovals in half, creating a pocket, gently pressing edges to seal.
6. Evenly space pastry pockets on prepared pans. Brush tops with egg yolk mixture; let stand for 5 minutes. Brush again with egg yolk mixture; let stand for 5 minutes more. Using a small sharp knife, gently score

desired design into top of pastry pocket. Using a wooden pick, poke 4 to 5 holes discreetly in design to vent.

7. Bake, one pan at a time, until pastry pockets are puffed and golden brown, about 15 minutes, rotating pans once halfway. Remove from oven; brush with syrup mixture. Bake for 1 minute more. Let cool on pans on wire racks for at least 15 minutes. Serve warm or at room temperature.

**We used Dufour Classic Puff Pastry.*

GINGER-CARDAMOM KOUIGN-AMANN

Makes 12

¾ cup whole milk, room temperature
1 large egg
1¾ teaspoons instant yeast
3 cups bread flour
2¼ cups granulated sugar, divided
15 tablespoons unsalted butter, room temperature and divided, plus more for greasing pan
2¼ teaspoons kosher salt
¾ teaspoon ground ginger
¼ teaspoon ground cardamom

1. In the bowl of a stand mixer, whisk together milk, egg, and yeast by hand. Using the dough hook attachment, add flour, ¼ cup sugar, 2 tablespoons butter, and salt, and beat at low speed until dough comes together, about 1 minute, stopping to scrape down sides of bowl. (Dough may still look shaggy at this point.) Continue beating at low speed until dough pulls away from sides of bowl and passes the windowpane test (see Notes*), about 5 minutes, stopping to scrape down sides of bowl and dough hook as needed.

2. Spray a large bowl with cooking spray. Turn out dough onto a very lightly floured surface, and shape into a smooth ball. Place dough in bowl, turning to grease top. Cover and let rise in a warm, draft-free place (75°) until dough is nearly doubled in size and holds an indent when poked, about 2 hours.

3. On a sheet of parchment paper, draw a 6.5-inch square. Turn parchment over; place remaining 13 tablespoons butter on parchment. Spread butter evenly and shape into a straight-sided square; wrap in parchment and plastic wrap. (If butter gets too soft to work with, refrigerate for 5 minutes before continuing.)

4. Punch down dough, and on a lightly floured surface, roll into a 10-inch square. Line a sheet pan with parchment paper; lightly dust with flour. Place dough on prepared pan. Cover tightly with plastic wrap (to ensure dough does not dry out); refrigerate dough and butter square overnight.

5. Freeze dough for 15 minutes. Let butter block stand at room temperature until pliable, 10 to 15 minutes.

6. On a lightly floured surface, place chilled dough with one corner pointing toward you. Unwrap butter block, and place in center of dough rectangle, straight sides perpendicular to dough corners. Fold dough edges over to enclose butter block, pinching seams to seal. Roll dough into a 24x10-inch rectangle. Fold dough into thirds along long side like a letter; wrap dough in plastic wrap and freeze until chilled, 5 to 15 minutes.

7. On a lightly floured surface, place dough with one long side closest to you; roll into a 24x10-inch rectangle. Fold dough into thirds along long side like a letter; rotate 90 degrees. Repeat this rolling and folding process once more, freezing for 5 to 15 minutes, as needed, if dough gets too soft. Wrap in plastic wrap, and refrigerate for 45 minutes.

8. In a medium bowl, stir together remaining 2 cups sugar, ginger, and cardamom.

9. Coat a work surface with ½ cup sugar mixture. Transfer dough to work surface, and roll into a 24x10-inch rectangle. (Turn dough over, as needed, to help gain traction while rolling.) Sprinkle dough with another ½ cup sugar mixture, and fold into thirds along long side, like a letter. (If dough starts to feel too soft, freeze until chilled, 5 to 15 minutes.) Sprinkle work surface with another ½ cup sugar mixture. Roll dough into a 24x10-inch rectangle, and sprinkle with remaining ½ cup sugar mixture. Cut dough into 4-inch squares, discarding or reserving scraps for another use (see Notes**). Turn squares; fold in corners of each square to center, pressing center firmly.

10. Preheat oven to 375°. Place a rimmed baking sheet in oven to catch any butter drips. Generously butter a 12-cup muffin pan.

11. Transfer folded squares to prepared muffin cups. Cover with plastic wrap, and let rise at room temperature for 20 minutes. Place muffin pan on baking sheet in oven. Bake until sugar starts to turn golden, about 25 minutes. Using a small offset spatula, immediately remove from pan; serve warm or let cool to room temperature on a wire rack. Kouign-amann are best enjoyed the same day.

Notes:

**Test dough for proper gluten development using the windowpane test. Pinch off (don't tear) a small piece of dough. Slowly pull the dough out from the center. If the dough is* *ready, you will be able to stretch it until it's thin and translucent like a windowpane. If the dough tears, it's not quite ready.*

***Sugary dough scraps are delicious when baked. Twist together remaining pieces, and roll the twists into a spiral shape, tucking loose end underneath. Place on a parchment-lined baking sheet; cover and let rise at room temperature for 20 minutes. Bake at 375° until sugar starts to turn golden, 20 to 25 minutes.*

ESCARGOT AU CHOCOLAT

Makes 16

3½ to 3¾ cups all-purpose flour
3½ tablespoons granulated sugar
3 tablespoons Dutch process cocoa powder, sifted
3½ teaspoons kosher salt
¼ cup plus 1 tablespoon unsalted butter, softened and divided
2¼ teaspoons instant yeast
1¼ cups plus 1 tablespoon cool water (60°), divided
¾ cup Cocoa Almond Cream (recipe follows)
¾ cup finely chopped bittersweet chocolate baking bars
1 large egg
Confectioners' sugar, for dusting

1. In the bowl of a stand mixer fitted with the dough hook attachment, place 3½ cups flour, sugar, cocoa, salt, 1 tablespoon butter, and yeast. Add 1¼ cups cool water, and beat at low speed until moistened, 1 to 2 minutes, scraping down sides of bowl. Increase mixer speed to medium, and beat until a smooth, tacky, elastic dough forms, 6 to 8 minutes, adding remaining ¼ cup flour, 1 tablespoon at a time as needed if dough is too sticky.
2. Spray a large bowl with cooking spray; place dough in bowl, turning to grease top. Cover bowl with plastic wrap, and let rise let rise in a warm, draft-free place (75°) for 1 hour. (Dough will nearly double and will hold an indent when poked.)
3. On a lightly floured surface, punch down dough and roll into a 10-inch square. Wrap dough in plastic wrap, and freeze for 30 minutes, turning halfway through. Meanwhile, microwave remaining ¼ cup butter on high in 10-second intervals until melted; let stand at room temperature to cool.
4. On a lightly floured surface, roll dough

into a 15x10-inch rectangle, with one short side facing you; brush with a third of melted butter (approximately 4 teaspoons). Fold dough into thirds along long sides like a letter; turn dough 90 degrees. Repeat this rolling, buttering, and folding process once more; wrap in plastic wrap, and refrigerate for 20 minutes. Place chilled dough rectangle on a lightly floured surface with one short side facing you; roll into a 15x10-inch rectangle, brush with remaining third of butter, and folding into thirds along the long sides like a letter; wrap tightly in plastic wrap, and refrigerate for 30 minutes more.

5. Preheat oven to 375°. Line 2 rimmed baking sheets with parchment paper.

6. On a very lightly floured surface, roll dough into a 28x12-inch rectangle, with one long side facing you. (This will take some effort, and some small tears may occur in dough layers.) Using a large offset spatula, spread Cocoa Almond Cream evenly over dough, leaving a ½-inch border on one long side. Sprinkle evenly with chopped chocolate. Roll dough tightly, jelly roll style; pinch seams to seal, and gently roll and shape dough into an evenly thick 28-inch log, as needed. Using a serrated knife, cut crosswise into 16 slices (each approximately 1¾-inches thick), wiping knife clean between cuts. Place slices, cut sides down, at least 2 inches apart on prepared pans.

7. Cover with plastic wrap, and let rise until puffed and nearly doubled in size, 40 to 60 minutes.

8. In a small bowl, whisk together egg and remaining 1 tablespoon cool water. Brush egg wash over pastry rounds.

9. Bake, one pan at a time, until puffed and an instant-read thermometer inserted in centers registers 190°, 12 to 14 minutes. Serve warm or transfer to a wire rack and let cool to room temperature. Dust with confectioners' sugar before serving.

COCOA ALMOND CREAM

Makes approximately ¾ cup

3 tablespoons unsalted butter, room temperature
½ cup superfine almond flour
3½ tablespoons granulated sugar
1 large egg
1 tablespoon Dutch process cocoa powder, sifted
¾ teaspoon almond extract
½ teaspoon vanilla bean paste
¼ teaspoon kosher salt

In a large bowl, stir butter until creamy. Add almond flour, sugar, egg, cocoa, almond extract, vanilla bean paste, and salt; whisk until well combined. Use immediately or press a sheet of plastic wrap against surface and refrigerate for up to 4 days. Microwave refrigerated almond cream in 5-second intervals just until easily spreadable.

"It's such happiness when people get together."

—Jane Austen

Space for Celebration

Gathering together brings great blessings, but leaning into your entertaining style, housing situation, and stage of life can enhance the joy of serving as host. First, consider your personality. Do you prefer filling the house with as many friends as possible or keeping things cozy with a few special guests? Planning ahead or extending an impromptu invitation? Handling every detail or dividing responsibilities? Dressing up for a formal affair or creating a casual and carefree ambience?

Next, assessing your abode helps in planning the most appropriate types of events for your space, as well as finding creative solutions for working around any limitations. For example, one woman who enjoyed having ladies' luncheons in her grand family home discovered, when she moved to cozier quarters, that she could still welcome larger groups with pretty, individually prepared basket lunches. Finally, setting personal expectations that align with your season of life can ensure that the party is fun for everyone, including you as the host.

Whether honoring a milestone moment or appreciating the beauty of ordinary days, opportunities abound for opening our homes to loved ones. Looking through the *Victoria* lens, we find inspiration for commemorating holidays, birthdays, and everyday occasions.

Beginning with New Year's Day, the calendar affords opportunities for welcoming loved ones to observe a variety of holidays. Lending warmth to winter, Valentine's Day reminds us to fill our homes with sweetness. Appreciating love in its many forms encourages not only planning thoughtful surprises for one's beloved but also celebrating other close relationships. A few of my favorite past gatherings include family breakfasts with heart-shaped pastries, an easy weeknight dinner with girlfriends where each guest brought a grazing board, and more formal Valentine tea parties.

"'TWAS EASTER-SUNDAY. THE FULL-BLOSSOMED TREES FILLED ALL THE AIR WITH FRAGRANCE AND WITH JOY."

—Henry Wadsworth Longfellow

Whether cheering hometown heroes as they parade down Main Street or watching with rapt attention as fireworks illuminate the night sky, Independence Day is a holiday to enjoy to the full with friends and neighbors. Let the simple gifts of summertime—glorious golden sunshine, ruby-hued watermelon, and gentle coastal breezes—set the tone for relaxed entertaining.

Since our first opportunity to welcome family for Thanksgiving, we have served as hosts many times. Over the years, I have found a few secrets to success. First, preparation is key, both for the occasion and for my heart. A few weeks before the gathering, I make ahead any dishes that freeze well, press linens and tackle a litany of household tasks, and begin praying for each person on the guest list. After the meal, going around the table to let each person share words of gratitude becomes a meaningful, heartfelt tradition.

"CHRISTMAS IS A TIME WHEN WE BRING FRIENDS AND FAMILY INTO OUR HOMES TO BE REFRESHED."

—Sally Clarkson

Marking a loved one's birthday is to say, in essence, "I cherish the day you were born as one of significance." The most important aspect of making such an occasion special is to tailor the celebration to the tastes and preferences of the recipient. If festivities include dessert, let me recommend Lavender Chamomile Tiered Cake, a recipe developed in the *Victoria* test kitchens.

LAVENDER CHAMOMILE TIERED CAKE

Makes 1 (8-inch) layer and 1 (6-inch) layer

1 cup whole milk
6 chamomile tea bags
1 cup unsalted butter, room temperature
3¾ cups granulated sugar
¾ cup vegetable oil
6 large eggs, room temperature
2 tablespoons vanilla extract
5¾ cups unbleached cake flour
4 teaspoons baking powder
1½ tablespoons culinary lavender
1¾ teaspoons kosher salt
¾ cup cold heavy whipping cream
Classic Vanilla Buttercream (recipe follows)
Edible flowers*
Fresh herbs
6 wooden dowels

1. In a medium saucepan, heat milk over medium-low heat just until bubbles start to form around edges (do not boil). Remove from heat and add tea; cover and let steep for 20 minutes. Remove bags, squeezing to extract as much liquid as possible. Let cool to room temperature.

2. Preheat oven to 350°. Spray 3 (8-inch) round cake pans and 3 (6-inch) round cake pans with baking spray with flour. Line bottoms of pans with parchment paper.

3. In the bowl of a stand mixer fitted with the paddle attachment, beat butter and sugar at medium speed until fluffy, 4 to 5 minutes, stopping to scrape down sides of bowl. Reduce speed to medium-low and pour oil in a slow, steady stream until incorporated. Increase speed to medium, and add eggs, one at a time, beating well after each addition. Beat in vanilla extract.

4. In a medium bowl, whisk together flour, baking powder, lavender, and salt. With mixer at low speed, gradually add flour mixture to butter mixture alternately with chamomile-infused milk, beginning and ending with flour mixture, beating just until combined after each addition.

5. In a separate medium bowl, whisk cold cream until soft peaks form. Fold into cake batter in two additions. Divide batter evenly among prepared pans (approximately 2½ cups in each 8-inch pan and 1½ cups in each 6-inch pan), smoothing tops. Run a wooden pick through batter to remove any large air bubbles.

6. Working in batches, bake cakes until tops are dry and golden brown and a wooden pick inserted into centers comes out clean, 20 to 25 minutes (see Note.) Let cool in pans for 10 minutes. Remove from pans and let cool completely on wire racks.

7. Level cooled cakes, if desired. Place 1 cooled 8-inch cake on a cake board. Spread 1½ cups Classic Vanilla Buttercream over top. Top with second 8-inch cake and spread 1½ cups frosting over top. Spread

1 cup buttercream over top and sides of cake to create a crumb coat; refrigerate for 10 minutes.

8. Place 1 cooled 6-inch cake on a cake board trimmed to the size of cake layer. Spread 1 cup frosting over top. Top with a second 6-inch cake and spread 1 cup frosting over top. Spread ½ cup frosting over top and sides of cake to create a crumb coat; refrigerate for 10 minutes.

9. Spread 2 cups frosting over top and sides of chilled 8-inch cake. Trimming to fit stems as needed, gently press desired flowers and herbs into sides of cake. Refrigerate until frosting is firm, about 20 minutes. Repeat process on chilled 6-inch cake with remaining 1 cup frosting and additional flowers and herbs. Refrigerate until buttercream is firm, about 20 minutes.

10. To assemble: Gently imprint 8-inch cake with a 6-inch cake board in the center. This will act as a guide for wooden dowels and top tier placement. Trim wooden dowels to height of assembled 8-inch cake. Gently insert dowels into 8-inch cake, spacing approximately 1½ inches from edge of 6-inch cake imprint. Carefully place chilled 6-inch cake on top of 8-inch cake where imprint was previously made. Arrange remaining flowers and herbs around edge of 6-inch cake to hide cake board, if needed. Refrigerate until ready to serve.

Note: While baking cake layers, leave remaining batter at room temperature.

**We used flowers from Gourmet Sweet Botanicals, gourmetsweetbotanicals.com.*

CLASSIC VANILLA BUTTERCREAM

Makes approximately 10½ cups

4 cups unsalted butter, softened
1½ teaspoons kosher salt
15 cups confectioners' sugar
1½ cups heavy whipping cream, room temperature
3 teaspoons vanilla extract

In the bowl of a stand mixer fitted with the paddle attachment, beat butter and salt at medium speed until creamy, 1 to 2 minutes, stopping to scrape down sides of bowl. With mixer at low speed, gradually add confectioners' sugar alternately with cream, beginning and ending with confectioners' sugar, beating until fluffy and combined. Beat in vanilla extract. Use immediately.

LED BY A SINGLE GRACE NOTE

Although grand occasions certainly have their place on the social calendar, setting the mark too high for everyday entertaining can result in missed opportunities for welcoming people into our lives. Time does not always allow for a full expression of hospitality, but connections can still be forged if we let singular moments of beauty open the door.

My mother-in-law once planned a garden party to commemorate the blooming of her evening primrose. Guests gathered at twilight to enjoy dinner, and as darkness fell, they were encouraged to pull their chairs into a circle around the plant. A few in the group found the request amusing, but questioning looks quickly turned to gasps of amazement as a profusion of blossoms began unfurling their petals. Years later, even the most reluctant comers still reminisce about the spectacular nature show they observed.

The ease of this fête encourages me to celebrate similar treasures. Discovering a new recipe for blackberry cobbler can prompt an invitation to a neighbor for dessert. Fresh-plucked heirloom tomatoes bursting with summer flavor, an antique transferware platter perfect for displaying bakery goods, the enchanting hours of late afternoon that render the landscape luminous—even the simplest of gifts can inspire us to reach out, if only we understand that joy is amplified when it is shared.

As we come to the end of this volume, I hope that you have found encouragement for creating a place of belonging—an abode that nurtures your spirit, serves as a haven for its inhabitants, welcomes friends, and always brims with love. I leave you with the words of an Irish blessing:

> "May love and laughter light your days and warm your heart and home.
> May good and faithful friends be yours, wherever you may roam.
> May peace and plenty bless your world with joy that long endures.
> May all life's passing seasons bring the best to you and yours."

CREDITS & RESOURCES

The Gracious Home: Cultivating a Spirit of Welcome
Editor: Melissa Lester
Creative Director, Lifestyle: Melissa Sturdivant Smith
Senior Features Editor: Leslie Bennett Smith
Features Editor: Lydia McMullen
Administrative Senior Art Director: Tracy Wood Franklin
Editorial Assistant: Audra Shalles
Senior Copy Editor, Lifestyle: Rhonda Lee Lother
Senior Digital Imaging Specialist: Delisa McDaniel

CONTRIBUTING PHOTOGRAPHERS

JENNY BOHANNON: pages 8, 46, 50–53, and 106–107
JANE HOPE: pages 10, 12, 17, 30, 32, and 35–36
MAC JAMIESON: pages 6, 66–71, 86, 100–102, 116, and 118–119
JOHN O'HAGAN: pages 4–5, 23-26, 72-73, 114, and 125–127
KATE SEARS: pages 88, 90–93, 120, 122–123, and 131–133
CYNTHIA SHAFFER: pages 94 and 105
MARCY BLACK SIMPSON: pages 2, 40, 43, 80, 82–83, 87, 110–113, and 146–147
STEPHANIE WELBOURNE STEELE: Cover, pages 20–21, 39, 44, 48–49, 54–65, 74, 76, 78–79, 84, 96, 98–99, 108–109, 128–129, 135–136, 138, 140, 142, 144, 148–157, 160, 164, and back cover
YUKIE MCCLEAN: pages 6, 80, 102, 116, 118–119, and 146–147
ANN MONFORE: pages 66–67
DARIEN ROZELL: pages 110–111
SHARON SANTONI: pages 30, 32, and 35–36
KRISTIE SHELTON: page 87
MALLORY SMITH: pages 144 and 154–155
MELISSA STURDIVANT SMITH: pages 2, 20–21, 39, 43–44, 54–65, 74, 76, 78–79, 84, 86, 100–101, 108–109, 112–113, 122, 128–129, 142, 144, 148–157, 160, 164, and back cover
KATHLEEN VARNER: pages 82–83
JANIE WILLIS: cover and pages 48–49
TINA YARAGHI: pages 58–61

CONTRIBUTING STYLISTS

CAROLYN AIKEN: pages 88–93
LIDY BAARS: pages 94 and 105
JENNY BOHANNON: pages 8, 46, 50–53, and 106–107
SIDNEY BRAGIEL: pages 66–71, 87, 96, 98–99, 110–111, 135–136, 138, and 140
MISSIE NEVILLE CRAWFORD: pages 82–83
COURTNEY DAVEY: pages 44 and 62–65
ANNE DUTCHER: pages 72–73
MARY FINCH: page 40
ANSLEY FORSBERG: pages 4–5, 114, and 125–127
KELLI DELANEY KOT: pages 108–109
MARSHA MASON: pages 23–26
NICOLA BATHIE MCLAUGHLIN: pages 54–57 and 128–129

CONTRIBUTING RECIPE DEVELOPERS AND FOOD STYLISTS

BECCA CUMMINS: pages 156–159
KATIE MOON DICKERSON: pages 156–159
KATHLEEN KANEN: pages 156–159
TRICIA MANZANERO: pages 134–141
VANESSA ROCCHIO: pages 134–141

WITH SPECIAL THANKS

Below is a listing of properties, products, and companies featured in this book.

Cover and pages 48–49: Special thanks to Janie Willis of Jane Marsden Antiques and Interiors, marsdenantiques.com.
Pages 2 and 43: Linens from Pandora de Balthazár Fine Linens; pandoradebalthazar.com.
Pages 4–5, 114, and 124–127: To learn more about Ansley Forsberg, visit @becomingbuckhead on Instagram.
Pages 8–9, 46, 50–53, and 106–107: To learn more about Jenny Bohannon and Tallwood Country House, visit @tallwoodcountryhouse on Instagram.
Page 21: Linens from Soft Surroundings; softsurroundings.com.
Pages 22–28: For more information about Marsha Mason, visit @marshamason2 on Instagram. For more information

about artist Jo Farris, visit jo-farris.com. Gullatte Associates, Inc., 1019 Broadway Street, #5, Columbus, GA.
Pages 30 and 32–36: For more information about Sharon Santoni, visit sharonsantoni.com.
Page 40: Mary McCollister Finch, interior decorator, Mary McCollister and Company, Birmingham, AL, marymcco@aol.com.
Pages 44 and 62–65: To learn more about Courtney Davey, follow @tuftandtrim on Instagram or visit tuftandtrim.com. Flowers courtesy of Grace Rose Farm, gracerosefarm.com. Pillows from Stuck on Hue; stuckonhue.com.
Pages 54–57 and 128–129: Special thanks to homeowner Nicola Bathie McLaughlin. Learn more about Nicola on Instagram at @nicolabathiemclaughlin and Nicola Bathie Jewelry at nicolabathie.com and on Instagram at @nicolabathiejewelry.
Pages 58–61: For more information about The Enchanted Home, visit enchantedhome.com or @theenchantedhome on Instagram.
Pages 72–73: Anne Dutcher Interiors, LLC, annedutcherinteriors.com. Artifice, Inc., artificeinc.com.
Pages 76 and 78–79: Antiquity Acres can be rented through Airbnb, airbnb.com/rooms/20941284.
Pages 82–83: Antique lounge chair; from Tricia's Treasures, triciastreasures.us.
Page 84: Learn more about Vilcy Nelson and Specialties by V by following @specialtiesbyv on Instagram. Shop her linens at etsy.com/shop/specialtiesbyvshop.
Pages 86 and 164: Carolina Elizabeth Fine Art Studio; carolinaelizabeth.com.
Page 87: Learn more about Kristie Shelton at kristieshelton.com and @kristiesheltonstudios on Instagram. Shop Kristie's art prints at etsy.com/shop/KristieSheltonStudio.
Pages 88–93: For more information about Carolyn Aiken, visit warrengrovegarden.blogspot.com or @aikenhouseandgardens on Instagram.
Pages 94 and 105: To learn more about Lidy Baars and FrenchGardenHouse, visit frenchgardenhouse.com or @frenchgardenhouse on Instagram.
Pages 100–101: Special thanks to Maison de France Antiques, 1304 8th Street, Leeds, AL.
Page 102: Castleton USA: Castleton Rose Footed Cup & Saucer Set; Hutschenreuther: Richelieu Flat Cup & Saucer Set; Royal Albert: Serena Footed Cup & Saucer Set; Shelley: Dainty Blue Flat Cup & Saucer Set, Spode: Irene Footed Cup & Saucer Set; from Replacements, Ltd., replacements.com.
Pages 108–109: To learn more about Kelli Delaney Kot, visit kdhamptons.com or @kdhamptons on Instagram.
Pages 110–111: To learn more about Darien Rozell and Pantry Hill, visit pantryhill.com or @pantry.hill on Instagram.
Pages 130–133: Berry Manor Inn, 81 Talbot Avenue, Rockland, ME, berrymanorinn.com.
Pages 134–141: Mottahedeh: Cornflower Lace Tea Cup & Saucer, Cornflower Lace Dinner Plate, Cornflower Lace Dessert Plate; mottahedeh.com.
Pages 144 and 154–155: Special thanks to homeowner Mimi Ritchie. Interior design by Mallory Smith Interiors, @mallorysmithinteriors on Instagram.
Pages 148–149: Adelene Simple Cloth: Chalk Fabric in Viola; adelenesimplecloth.com. Royal Copenhagen: Blue Fluted Half Lace Bowl, Blue Fluted Half Lace Cup and Saucer, Blue Fluted Half Lace Cake Stand; royalcopenhagen.com.
Pages 152–153: Spode: Indian Tree (Orange Rust, Scallop, Red Trim) Place Setting, Indian Tree (Orange Rust, Scallop, Red Trim) Tureen No Lid; from Replacements, Ltd., replacements.com.
Pages 156–157: Sadek: Amore Creamer, Amore Teapot & Lid, Amore Salad/Dessert Plate, Amore Flat Cup & Saucer Set; from Replacements, Ltd., replacements.com.
Page 160: Arte Italica: Sofia Water/Wine Glass, Merletto Antique Dinner Plate, Merletto Antique Cereal Bowl, Linens; arteitalica.com.
Page 164: Pillows from Le Lis Home, @le.lis.home on Instagram, lelishome.etsy.com. Mayflower Wallpaper: Marble Floral MF10001; mayflowerwallpaper.com. Throw from Three Sheets; @threesheetslinens on Instagram.

BELLE MAISON
INTERMEZZO